4 Front Doors of
a Successful
BUSINESS

PAUL GAGLIA

PAGE PUBLISHING
Conneaut Lake, PA

First originally published by Page Publishing 2024

ISBN 979-8-89157-249-2 (pbk)
ISBN 979-8-89157-264-5 (digital)

Printed in the United States of America

Acknowledgments

I must express my thanks to my parents, Roland and Vilma Gaglia, for providing me with all the support in a positive atmosphere with an accent on a healthy approach to life.

Not many people have had the honor of working for over twenty years seven days a week with their father as a constant mentor and their mother who was the ultimate positive influencer. And I thank them for that.

I also want to thank my wife, Donna, for standing by me for the good and the not so good without wavering.

Appreciation is also to be given to my sister Toni and her husband, John, who have always been my sounding boards and detectives, making sure my paths were the right paths.

Finally, I want to thank all the employees throughout the years who adopted my philosophies and acted on them positively, creating a very positive, memorable experience for all who crossed our paths.

Introduction

The overall goal of this book is to enrich the people who read it and to touch them with a sense of comfort and gratification that will have a positive impact on their personal and professional approach to the future.

Although this book is predominantly based on a garden center, it is definitely able to be adapted to any business enterprise. It can be a retail establishment, a manufacturing establishment, or a professional establishment, to name a few. A few tweaks and some innovative thinking outside the box will guide you to a business unsurpassed in your industry and field.

I promise that when you enact these principles, you will be creating a memorable experience of value to your customers. You will be giving your customers outstanding service and top-quality products and workmanship in a timely, professional manner, all in a satisfying and pleasurable atmosphere.

Your long-term plan will be to give continued growth and expansion by giving top-of-the-line products, service, and value through continued investment in talent, innovation, education, team building, communication, honest standards, and expectations and by continually measuring, focusing, and refocusing your positive movement.

Remember:

1. You have been given a bag of cement and a bucket of water. You can either build a stepping stone or a stumbling block. The choice is (and always has been) yours. [Fill in your name], it's a stepping stone or a stumbling block. *Nothing else. It's up to you!*

2. *Life!* The grass is not greener on the other side. It's not even greener on this side *unless you water it!*

3. And finally, the system is the solution. The system runs the business, *and the people run the system!*

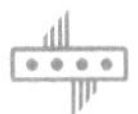

A number of years ago, a very good friend of mine—let's call him Mike Eck or Eck for short—asked if I could help a struggling garden center out by offering some constructive suggestions. This sounded good to me, but I wanted to first visit the store acting as a customer and later return with Eck for formal introductions.

But before I go any further, I must explain my personal and professional background that would qualify my ability to offer any type of constructive suggestions.

I'll start somewhere near the beginning on a personal basis that leads to my professional offerings.

At a very young age, I would say when I was ten or eleven, every year my father would compile a "summer to-do list" for me to accomplish before I was permitted to go out and play baseball etc. with my friends. The summer to-do list consisted of various outdoor and indoor tasks. The outdoor tasks were things such as hand-edging all the hedges, trees, and shrub beds throughout the entire yard, front and back. He would lay out a string line that I was to follow, and he would inspect my progress and quality every night when he came home from work. We would discuss in detail the work progress and quality. This, I now believe, was the beginning of my "eye for detail" or "critical eye." He would point out my shortcomings and explain how to correct them, and we also discussed my strengths. Then we—I mean he—would devise a new plan of action, which usually required me to slow down and this time follow the string line. I caught on quickly, so I didn't have to double- or even triple-work, and I could finish my chores faster and go play ball or whatever with my friends. Some of my other to-do list items were—and I won't go into detail—to prune the hedges, which went around three sides of our backyard; prune the shrubs; and cut the low branches and suckers on the trees. I was to pattern-cut the grass weekly or as needed, which was when my dad said it needed done, changing direction every week so the grassblades do not get damaged; rake up or bag the grass clippings; and dispose of them in the compost pile. I would trim or hand-prune the grass away from buildings, walkways, and garden or shrub or hedge edges. Now you must remember this was in 1960–61. The Weedwacker or even the battery-operated hand grass or shrub pruners were not invented in my world yet. I used the old-fashioned mechanical scissor-style hand and hedge pruners (this helped build your forearm muscles).

Let's jump ahead to age sixteen. I know this because I was a licensed driver at this time. My dad, while reading the Sunday paper, saw an ad at a local garden center that they were having a sale for mountain ash trees. The sale was for a one-inch-caliper mountain ash at a cost of $1.99 (remember, it was 1966). And Dad always liked the mountain ash trees. They were a shapely tree that was medium height and width, and they had white flowers and orange fruit. So my dad decided that I was going to buy one of these mountain ash trees and install it in a specific spot in our backyard. So we ventured out in the backyard, and after a great deal of analyzing the sunset direction over our patio, he found the spot, so we put a stake in the ground where I was to plant the tree. Then Dad explained in detail how I was going to plant the tree. We used a string line to define the area (Dad was big on string guides) and staked off the area of the circle I was to dig out. Dad also explained how deep I was to dig the hole. We went into the house and wrote the plan down with drawings and everything.

The next morning, I got up early, and I did as I was instructed. I dug a hole three feet in diameter and 1.5 feet deep, saving all the soil to use later after I add amendments to use as backfill. (The hole looked like an asteroid had landed in our backyard. But what did I know? It was my first planting.) After I completed this portion of the project, I got into my dad's Oldsmobile, and off I went to the local garden center. This was my first tree purchase and planting. Man, I was pumped! The night before, my dad and I wrote up a plan and diagram of the tree I was to purchase. It explained how to pick the best tree. It was to have a straight trunk; the first set of branches should be four feet off the pot, and the upper branches should be symmetrical, with a single leader branch going from the trunk straight up the middle to the top of the tree. I was ready. Armed with my notes, I felt very confident. On the list, Dad also wrote to buy some peat moss, a small bale, tree fertilizer, and a tree staking kit.

I was very diligent looking for the perfect tree. I walked up and down the mountain ash tree aisle, looking with a very perceptive eye. I looked at the trunk, the first branches, the leader branch, and the overall shape of the tree. This process was written on the instructions my dad prepared. As I was walking and looking, one tree kept saying, "Take me! Take me!" So I had to pick it. I did believe I found the perfect tree. It crossed off all my dad's specifications. Boy, was he going to be happy! I know I was satisfied.

Excitement! I proceeded to the checkout counter with the tree, peat moss, tree fertilizer, and tree staking kit. A proud walk, I might add. I carefully loaded the tree, taking care not to damage any branches or leaves. I rested the tree trunk on the peat moss bale and laid the tree fertilizer on the back floor of the car along with the tree staking kit. I now hit the road, excited, armed, and dangerous, ready to do my first planting. And it was a tree no less!

When I arrived back at the house, I carefully unloaded everything and carried it to the now mammoth-looking hole I had dug an hour or two ago. Following my dad's explicit planting instructions, I first mixed peat moss into the existing soil and placed the mix in the center of the hole, tamping the soil mix lightly as I built the mound. I did this so the tree would not sink and possibly die because it was planted too deep. I then took the pot off the bottom of the tree, and I gently pulled the roots loose. Then I proceeded to mix the peat moss, existing soil, and tree fertilizer (as my dad's detailed instructions stated) to finish the planting process. When that task was completed, I took the tree staking kit to make sure the tree would stay straight during its first season of root development. I used my dad's two-foot level to make sure the tree trunk was straight all the way around as I installed each tree stake. This was another case of "eye for detail" or "the critical eye," of which I was totally unaware I was being trained to develop. The finishing touches to the planting process was to place the remaining peat moss over the top of the entire planting bed area. This was for water retention. My first planting was a success! When my dad came home from work later that day, we both went out back to inspect my handiwork. As my dad walked around the tree, with his hand on his chin and a nonfilter Chesterfield cigarette leaning out of his mouth, I stood there in anxious anticipation. He stopped walking, looked at me, and said, "Great job, son." Wow, I was so relieved and happy. I passed my first planting test! Yay for me! This success spurred me on to other similar projects and spawned a love of planting and lawn care that would ultimately lead me into my future career.

Also, at age sixteen, I wanted a car, but we didn't have enough room in our present driveway to accommodate another vehicle. So my dad suggested that if I wanted a car, I could dig out an area adjacent to the existing driveway. He would then consider me having the opportunity to get a car. I readily agreed. So when I agreed, we headed out to the driveway armed with my dad's trusty string line, stakes, a small sledge, and tape measure to stake out the area I was to dig up to possibly secure my place in the car family ownership, an honor every sixteen-year-old dreamed about. I got up very early the next day, and after a hearty breakfast, I grabbed my dad's trusty pick, spade, and flat shovel and our old steel-wheeled wheelbarrow and started my mapped-out parking spot design laid out the night before. Man, I didn't realize that compacted dirt, when loosened, expanded, but with a goal of possible vehicle ownership entrenched in my mind, I continued. Pick, dig, scrape, load, and wheel to the backyard (dump), neatly placing and spreading the dirt under the freshly edged hedge beds. After three days of pick-dig-scrape-load-wheel-dump-spread, the project was complete. Now the dad inspection phase to see if it was going to be accepted or corrected came into play. After work that evening, Dad and I proceeded outside to the driveway for the inspection. Again, my dad walked around with his hand on his chin and puffing on a filterless Chesterfield cigarette. He went into the garage and came out with a tape measure and level, and we proceeded to measure, analyze, check the level, etc. After about half an hour of measuring, analyzing, level checking, etc., he stopped, turned to me, and said, "I think we need a wall in this area."

Well, that was the start of my second wall-building project in my life; the first one was when I was about nine or ten, when my dad had me rebuilding my grandfather's wall that had collapsed. That's a story for another day. Back in the '60s, there were very limited wall selections available. It was either used railroad tie walls or concrete block or brick walls or some derivative of the above mentioned basic walls. My dad's wall of choice was the mortared concrete block wall like we had throughout the existing driveway area. My heart sank. I had never mortared a wall before. What was I going to do? I discussed this matter with my dad (he already knew that), kind of pleading my case with him. After a few minutes in discussion and thought, Dad came up with a slightly different plan. He said, "You can use block, but you don't have to mortar it. This is a small four-block-high wall in areas about thirty feet long and tapering to one block on one side. But you will need to lean it back and mortar the block holes so no critters can get in. And you will need to backfill the wall with gravel." So I agreed. Boy, was I happy. I had dodged a real difficult task. Another adventure!

So the next day, I proceeded to build the wall according to my dad's instructions and sketch. One day, that was all it took! Now I'm ready for the car. When my dad came home that evening, we inspected my work, and it was approved with one more addition. Ugh, we need to add gravel in the new space to park the car on. So Dad ordered a load of gravel from our local garden center to be delivered the next day. As scheduled, the gravel was delivered, and I spread and hand-tamped it in that day. Now a car was all that was missing to occupy the new spot! That night, after work and the final inspection, we (my dad and I) decided that tomorrow, Saturday, my dad's day off, we would go car shopping at our local Oldsmobile car dealership. I was pumped!

The day had finally arrived! As we walked into the dealership, we were greeted by my dad's friend and salesperson, Mr. Rufft. My dad proceeded to explain to Mr. Rufft in detail our desires and needs. Mr. Rufft immediately said, "I have the car for you!" So we proceeded to the used-car lot, and lo and behold, there it was, my very first car and car payment, I might add. It was a beige 1962 Oldsmobile F-85 sedan! At the time, I would have taken anything. Later, with the help of my dad, I had it painted metallic burnt orange with a spray on vinyl top. I was soooo excited! After a test-drive, my dad said it was good, so we signed the papers, and off the lot I go to the new home of the F-85 in the new driveway I had prepared for her. How come all my cars are female? Oh well, she was mine. What a satisfying end to a growing experience.

Moving on now to my first professional landscape job. (My very first paying job was at a fast-food place, Burger Chef. I just recently found out that Hardee's Hamburgers bought Burger Chef. Another learning experience for another time.) It was my senior year in high school, and I was tired of flipping hamburgers. I was missing my passion for the outdoors and successfully creating, installing, and maintaining lawns, plants, and walls. So I stopped at our local garden/landscape center. Yes, the same one I have mentioned earlier. I always also wanted to drive trucks and operate machinery (like tractors, bucket machinery, etc.). So in my interview, I explained my interest in the industry and limited experience and desire to learn more, plus my desire to drive trucks and operate machinery. I thought I got this job. But to my surprise, I was not hired. I was crushed. I asked why, and the owner's reply was, "You're too small, son. You might get hurt." I came back with "I'm tough. I've played baseball and football, wrestled, and ran track in high school, and I was good in all of them." He still said no. So I left, a bit disillusioned. Back to hamburger flipping.

A few days later, a grounds maintenance company gave me a call. He was looking for help, so he stopped at the local garden center, and the owner gave him my application. We talked, and he said, "I'll give you a job on a trial basis." I accepted the job and the challenge. I was now excited about the job of my dreams. My starting wage was $2.50/hour. (It was 1967–68, so that was good pay at that time. I was getting paid $1.25/hour at Burger Chef. I doubled my pay. Not bad.) The job was tough, and so was the owner. But I was up to the challenges. I listened, performed, and learned the right way to do grounds maintenance. By midseason, I was the top guy. Ron, the owner, made me foreman over older men and guys who had worked for him longer. Lesson learned here: do not promote because of longevity; promote on work performance and leadership capabilities. I took the position, but I didn't get a raise. All I got was more responsibility. That really didn't matter to me because I was learning and I loved what I was doing. Everything was good until I found out that a friend of Ron's who was working part-time was getting paid $5.00/hour. What! I was the foreman responsible for running the crews, maintaining the vehicles and machinery, reporting to Ron, and getting the work done on a timely and professional manor. Every night I had to empty the trucks of the grass or other debris, clean the trucks inside and out, and maintain the mowers, plus make sure we have enough gasoline and chemicals for the next day's work and beyond.

All that for $2.50/hour while Ron's buddy got $5.00/hour to work part-time and go home at the end of the day doing no extra helping hand work. All I wanted was equal pay. Not more than him, just equal. Was that too much to ask? That was not happening on my watch. So I confronted Ron, and he came up with some lame excuses that I won't go into detail here. I told Ron that his reasoning was not acceptable to me and that I was giving my two-week notice. Ron asked what I was going to do, so I told him I was going to start my own grounds maintenance company. So off I go on another growth spurt.

This was a major stepping stone in the evolution of my professional career. I was stepping into the realm of the unknown. But as a wise man told me, a life-changing journey begins with a single step. And you must trust that other steps will follow. My first stop was home to tell my mom my plans. My mom was a very positive, upbeat eternal optimist. She was very excited of my aggressive, independent attitude. She always had my back. That afternoon, we devised a plan. First on the list, I needed to purchase some equipment so when I got to work, I was ready to go. So I ventured to our local garden center to purchase a good lawn mower and hand grass and hedge shears. At the time, the industry standards were nineteen-inch or twenty-four-inch Lawn-

Boy lawn mowers with a bag or two manual hand and hedge shears. So that was what I did. I bought a nineteen-inch push mower with an extra bag and the shears. You have to understand that these items were the standard for all grounds maintenance/landscape companies of this era. (The large walk-behind mowers and quality riding lawn mowers were either not invented yet or simply not of the quality a professional used. Also, the hand grass and hedge shears were all manual. The battery-operated or gasoline-operated were not available yet.)

When I returned home, my mom and I unboxed the mower and assembled it in the middle of our living room floor. Now what? Mom said, "Let's get you some business." So we ran a simple ad in a local newspaper. I believe the ad was "Grass Cutting," with our home phone number (cell phones were not in use yet). A few days later, we received a few phone calls from people interested in my services. We thought, *Great, that was easy!* Now the hard part. I had never gone on a bid or given an estimate. How hard could that be? So I ventured off to my local garden center for help. They gave me vague advice. It was, "How much do you want to make per hour? Well then, when you look at the job, how long do you think it will take to perform the work? There you go. That's your price." I thought, *Hmm, that's really simple. Now I'm ready to go on my first estimate.* I thanked them for all the help and insight, and I headed out on my very first estimate.

At this moment, I was confident, excited, and anxious all at the same time. As I was driving to the first estimate, I was thinking, *What am I going to say? How do I look? Do I look like a professional?* As I arrived at the first bid, my eyes surveyed the lawn. I thought it was pretty level. That was good. As I got to the front door, I thought the walk from the street to the front door didn't take too long. That was good too. I was creating my critical eye. I rang the doorbell, and the missus of the house greeted me. I introduced myself and explained my short but positive work experience. And I told her about my quick rise to being a foreman. She seemed to feel comfortable, and she proceeded to tell and show me the scope of the yard and what they wanted done. After our conversation, I excused myself so I could further analyze the work to determine a price. I walked the property at each corner, looking at the area. I really didn't know what I was looking at or for. But I thought I looked professional. I came back to the house and gave her the price. "I can do it for $25.00 per cut." She accepted my quote and asked when I could start. I told her I would be out tomorrow. She was happy, and so was I. As I was driving home to tell my mom my success, I realized I forgot one thing—I didn't have a truck. I thought for a minute and decided to use my car. Who would need a truck?

The next morning, I loaded my nineteen-inch Lawn-Boy, grass shears, and a box of plastic bags to bag up the grass clippings in order to not mess up my car. And off I went. I was happy and whistling about my very first independent project. I arrived at the job, pulled out the nineteen-inch Lawn-Boy mower and bag, and began to cut the grass. After several passes and emptying the bag several times, I thought to myself, *Is this the right lawn? Did the property get bigger overnight? Hmm?* Well, I bid it, and I was going to do the work, so I continued, determined to honor my agreement. Eight hours later, after cutting, bagging, and edging, I finally finished. The car was overloaded with bags. I had to put the mower in the front seat with me. Exhausted, I rang the doorbell, and the Mrs. came to the door with the cash to pay me. She marveled at how nice her lawn looked. I thanked her, but I explained that I grossly underbid her lawn, and I would not be able to continue to cut her lawn anymore. Then she proceeded to tell me the neighbor boy down the road would usually cut it with a riding lawn mower, but he did not bag or edge the grass, and she paid him $35.00. I thanked her, and off I went. I slept very well that night. This experience gave me many enlightening learning lessons: (1) learn how to bid, (2) don't depend on the industry to give you accurate or complete information, and (3) buy a truck.

As time passed, there were other estimating mistakes, or as the saying goes, "Some days you win, and some days you learn." So I would say I had many, many "learning experiences" ahead for me. I'll touch on the most important ones as we go ahead. This learning experience did not disillusion me; it gave me a greater determination to overcome my shortcomings. I learned I had to go back to the drawing board and devise a plan unique to me and my goals. I felt I should not follow the norm. I needed to think and act outside the box. And that was what I did and continued to do throughout my career. Also, I had my cheering section back home—my mom! She explained she was proud of me for completing the job with quality and for speaking up and admitting my mistake. She further said, "Take the positives: you completed the job with quality, you got compliments, and you got paid! Let's chalk this all up to a learning or a stepping-stone moment." She was sure I would encounter many more moments like this one, and they would all help me build a successful business and reach my ultimate goals. (Remember, I told you my mom was the eternal optimist.) I considered this not a failure but an opportunity to educate myself in the art of estimating and business acumen.

As time passed, my determined approach developed my own set of guidelines and rules through questioning, observation, reading many books, and going to numerous seminars. (The Internet was not available or built as it is today; it was still in the DOS stage. You had to write your own programs!) This was the start of my constant ever-changing evolution and tweaking of not only my estimating practices but also my total business philosophies. Change not for the sake of change but for the betterment of the overall company. I not only read, questioned, observed, or went to seminars for general business knowledge; I became a student and eventually a master of the industry.

Let's backtrack a bit in order to fully understand my educational and life experiences.

My father was a shoe store manager, promoted to a district manager and ultimately vice president. In my younger days, when my dad was a shoe store manager, he would take me to work with him to help in the store. I would "shift" stock for him. When he was receiving a shipment of shoes, we needed to make room for the new stock. There were specific stock numbers to all shoes, and they had to be in chronological or numerical order in order for the sales staff to find the shoes quickly. Many times, in order to make the proper amount of stock, you had to shift half of the stock in order to place the shoes in numerical order. Plus, you would have to put them in size order, from smallest to largest, from left to right. Kind of a thankless job but rewarding for the shifter once enough slots were made. Also, my dad would take me to "shoe shows." At the time, they were not held in large arenas or convention centers, because back in the late '50s and '60s, there were no such things like that built yet. So we would go to hotels and venture from room to room in order to see various vendors and their new designs. Plus, we (my dad and I) would talk to the salespeople (who also slept in these rooms) and negotiate pricing, availability, etc. I was a good student listener.

When I was older, in college and still landscaping, I worked as a shoe salesperson / stock person. This was to complement my landscape income. All these shoe memories helped me build my work ethic and analytical thought process, which I would use in my growing landscape business. I learned that as a salesperson, to be successful, one needed to be very knowledgeable, confident, and lighthearted. And that approach greatly helped ease tension. In other words, "sell yourself," and the end result will be positive. Plus, this would build customer loyalty.

Now more about my journey of growth and development. There were more events that molded my business future, which are keys to creating my philosophy through real-life and business events. By this time, I had acquired several grounds maintenance customers. I bought an old bread van for $400.00 and hand-painted it safety yellow and bright green. You could not miss the van. I had two employees (who I brought in as equal partners), plus more equipment. Things were going well. I had made friends with other grounds maintenance / landscape people. They were taking notice of my growth and quality work. We would share stories, but not secrets. Plus, I was now subcontracting the local garden center's planting jobs. Kind of a change of events. Remember, I was too small. I continued to underbid some projects I wasn't familiar with. One such project was my first dethatching project.

I met a customer, Mr. Ray, who was in need of a lawn dethatch. I had never heard of such a thing. So I went to my local hardware store. What was it? How do I do it? And what equipment should I use? They were somewhat helpful and sold me a manual dethatching rake. It was odd-looking, but they showed me how to use it. It seemed simple enough. So I went back to Mr. Ray and told him I could do the work for $50.00.

Again, like my first grass cut, this turned out to be a disaster! It took me two days to dethatch his lawn, and all I was getting was $50.00. I finished the job and went to get paid. Mr. Ray invited me in and asked how much he owed me. I said $50.00 like I told him. He went off on a tangent as he was writing the check. I was getting upset. Mr. Ray ripped the check out of his checkbook and handed it to me and said, "This is what that job is worth." Oh no, what was he paying me? I looked, and it was $250.00! What? I looked at him in total surprise. No one had ever done that before. He proceeded to tell me he liked me. He said from now on he was going on every bid with me, and together we would come up with a fair price. Mr. Ray further said at this rate I would never make it in business doing such dumb things like that. This was the first person who really and honestly helped me. We molded a friendship and working relationship that worked for a while. We would eventually drift apart, only to meet up a while later after Mr. Ray and my education.

In 1973, when I graduated from college, I was at a crossroads. Do I continue with my lawn maintenance business? Do I pursue a teaching career? Or do I do something completely different? I was not crazy about teaching, and I felt I didn't want to push a lawn mower for the rest of my life, especially in my senior years. So I decided

I wanted to be a sales representative for any type of wholesale goods. So I went to a job placement company for help. They taught me how to write up a proper résumé and how to present myself in interviews. Plus, they taught me to research a prospective employer. I was to learn as much as I could about them. This would show my interest in their company. I landed a job with Keebler, a cookie company. I received a company car, a gas card, and $7,000.00 salary per year. Not the best, but I felt it would be a stepping stone to my future. After several weeks of training with various sales reps, it was finally my chance to show my ability. They cut up all the other routes to create a route for me. It consisted of all the stores the sales reps didn't want to service for one reason or another. Long story short, I had my work cut out for me. I was excited even though I knew what I was getting. A challenge! I rose to the occasion. In six short months, I made my lackluster route into the number 1 route in the district.

What next? So I met with the district manager to find out my next step. He informed me that was where I'd be for a while. Then he asked, "What did you expect? What are you looking for?" My response was, "I want a new challenge, like a position like yours." His answer was, "I'm not going anywhere in the near future, so that's out of the question. Be content with where you are now." I excused myself, and as I was driving home and thinking about my future, I decided I was not going to waste my life putting cookies on a shelf. When I arrived home, I packed up all my Keebler material and loaded them into the Keebler car and drove back to the warehouse and resigned. I then went back to landscaping and never looked back. Keebler did teach me a few things I would never forget and would use in the future. I learned how to "front" shelves so they appeared full even if they weren't and how to use "shelf talkers" as a way to attract customers to my section of the cookie aisle. Finally, I learned I was a pretty good salesman.

Now I was ready to take on more work and move on from simply grounds maintenance to actual landscaping. Here, I met Mr. Bill, a condominium, restaurant, commercial builder. Mr. Bill took me into a new, exciting arena. One of his major contributions to me was his project note-taking system. Every meeting, write it down and put it in a folder to use as reference later. He was also giving us (yes, now it is us; my brother, father, and I joined forces) multiple projects, building my confidence. Mr. Bill also noticed I was wearing all the hats of a business owner and that I was becoming overwhelmed. So we, Mr. Bill and I, discussed my need to learn how to delegate. This took a lot of meetings with Mr. Bill and my dad and brother. Mr. Bill taught me to hire people to do the work I didn't really enjoy or I was not very good at. This was an eye-opener. My very first delegation was to have my brother run the projects, which he excelled in. And my father became my purchasing officer and private confidant. We brought my mom in as secretary/bookkeeper. And I oversaw all of them, plus I did all the project procurement and scheduling. As time went on, we grew larger, and we needed to add more people. My brother's wife came in as a receptionist/secretary/promotional attaché. And my younger brother, who was then eighteen and married, came in to help with design work and estimating, along with other duties. So some of the duties changed, and we needed to hire more people not related to help carry the added workload and lessen the stress of the existing workforce.

We held weekly and sometimes daily formal and often informal meetings. The informal meetings were always held at my mom and dad's house over a spaghetti dinner. Eat and talk shop the good old days. All the meetings, formal and informal, helped the business. We would discuss our shortcomings and make a plan of action to correct them. One major short fall was finance. We made a plan to visit local banks, looking for help. Dad found one bank willing to help us grow. It was a local two-office bank. Dad met with the bank president/owner, Mr. McDee, and laid out our growth plan. Mr. McDee was a great gentleman and forward thinker. After a few meetings, they (Dad and Mr. McDee) came to an agreement that was amicable to both parties. This plan was very novel, and I was never able to duplicate it again. It was a win-win agreement.

This is how it was structured. When we received an executed agreement from a general contractor, we would present it to Mr. McDee, and in return, Mr. McDee would advance us 50 percent of the total project. Of course, there was a modest interest rate. He would fund us this way for as many projects that we secured. We could come in as many times in any given day with new executed contracts, and he would fund them at the proper time, which was a few days before starting the project. The payment of the projects was key to the bank's involvement and security. Prior to executing the agreement, we would contact the general contractor's accounting department and tell them that when making a payment to us, they needed to make all checks payable to us and the bank. We called this an assignment of accounts. The hidden gem in this was, the general contractors paid us faster.

We would go to the bank with the checks and hand them to Mr. McDee for processing. He would take his 50 percent plus interest out first and then deposit the remaining funds into our account. Kind of a sweet deal. This deal worked great for our short-term funding. But I felt it wasn't enough. We also needed long-term funding to help us obtain and upgrade our vehicle and equipment needs. So this time, I went to Mr. McDee and asked what he could do for us in that area. He explained that what he was doing for us was adequate, and over time, we would benefit more this way. Well, at this time, I was an over-confident meathead. So I went out looking for a bank that would do both short-term and long-term financing. After knocking on many doors, I finally found a bank that said they would do both. This was a much-larger bank, and in my naive approach, bigger is better. Not true as you will see. I went to Mr. McDee, and I told him I found a bank that was willing to give us both types of funding. He warned me to be careful because that particular bank was notorious for overpromising and not following through on their promises. I thanked him for all his help over the years and concern, but my mind was made up, and off I went.

The first six months, everything was peachy. I had some long-term money with the promise of more to come in the future. And as promised, the "assignment" funds were funded as we negotiated. Then all of a sudden, the bank had a shake-up. Bank auditors were in the bank checking everything. They were looking for fraudulent banking deals. And this bank had a lot. Long story short, when they came to our deal, the auditors felt it was a clean deal, but it was too risky considering the bank's present underhanded dealing, and the bank was forced to call all our debit. This bank was eventually forced to merge with an even larger bank. Wow! What a blow to us. We were in dire straits. I went back to Mr. McDee with my tail between my legs and asked forgiveness. Mr. McDee was cordial but firm. He was not willing to help us out. What next? I was lost.

What next? We eventually went to the small business administration. After many months and mountains of paperwork, we did manage to receive funding. We also had to sign away our lives, pledge our homes, etc. Shortly after this funding, we hit a major project, which you will read about in the upcoming pages, that forced us into bankruptcy. Lesson learned: don't be an overconfident meathead and listen to the wiser council.

Just a little sidebar here. I have read many books, gone to countless seminars, and visited too many lending institutions and financial advisers who have any creative ways to obtain "growth funds." They all fit you into their very, very narrow boxes and conservative, conventional, pigeonhole, archaic practices. Ingenious practices such as Mr. McDee's and his bank. He was truly a creative pioneer in the banking industry that had been lost in today's financial arena, creatively light-years ahead of his time, which no one had ever duplicated.

We would discuss our victories and analyze how we could duplicate them and make them stronger. These changes, whether in personnel or policies and procedures, would ultimately help strengthen our overall business and develop our business strategies. This newfound confidence helped me to diversify the company into a painting company and concrete company to complement the landscaping. We moved the business from a nonunion company to a union company in order to take on larger projects. Here, I met Mr. Monaco. He taught me to not only write down my meetings with contractors but to also document our people's daily work performed. Thus, the birth of our daily foreman's report. I took one of Mr. Monaco's reports and retrofitted into our company. This became very beneficial down the road.

Over the years, our daily foreman's reports have come in handy in such areas as how the projects are progressing, employee performance or lack of performance, vehicle and equipment tracking, problems incurred on a site whether it is caused by another contractor, or our vehicles or equipment or materials, etc. In several cases, it helped in contract or performance disputes etc. One specific dispute arose when we were a sub-contractor on a giant government project. There was a financial penalty in the general contractor's agreement for not completing the project on time. The site developer, who, by the way, is the first contractor on any project, set the overall tone and pace of all sizable projects such as this one. They fell way behind on their work to the tune of six months. And there was a concrete timetable pre-set up due to a "grand opening" and pre-determined massive marketing agreements. This pushed every other subcontractor back also. We all tried to make up time, and we accomplished some, but not the entire six months. In general, the landscape contractor and fencing contractor were the final contractors having work left to complete the project. The site developer was the first on the site, and they received total compensation for their part of the project with no loss. In walked us and the fence contractor. With the project still behind, the general contractor was being penalized a substantial amount daily. We were not aware of such dealings, and both continued our best to complete it as fast as possible. When we finally completed our end of the project within our personal timetable, but not within the overall project timetable, the general contractor short-paid us and the fencing company. We were shorted $87,000.00, which was disastrous to us! We didn't know how much the fence contractor was short, but it was substantial.

We went to the general contractor, threatening a lawsuit etc. Their answer to us was, "Go ahead, sue us. It will take seven years to come up, and by then, you will be bankrupt!" What! So we did sue because we could not survive with such a financial hit like that. Time passed. We went into bankruptcy, but we were determined to have our day in court. So we, along with the bankruptcy court, pursued the case. Finally, depositions were called, our start to the day of reckoning. Long story short, my attorney and I came into the deposition with several storage boxes of foremen's reports. (Remember, this is about the absolute value of having documentation such as a foreman's report.) The attorney for the general contractor started off with a specific date that we were not on the job. So I dug into my foremen's reports, picked out the date, and read that we were actually on the project that day and that I had specific information as to what we did. This went on for several minutes. The opposing attorney finally asked what I had in the boxes. I told him they were foremen's reports for every day we were on their project. They adjourned for a bit, then returned to stop the deposition.

A few days later, they agreed to settle the dispute. Not being in charge of our future, the bankruptcy court settled for just enough to pay off our debts and cover their costs. We were left still broke. Prior to this, the bankruptcy court had a sale of all our equipment, etc. Our only satisfaction was that we beat them and again proved our determination.

Now it was winter. We were out of business, but not done. What were we going to do? We needed some sort of cash flow. My dad and mom were down. One of my brothers secured a job as a mechanic with one of his wife's relatives. I was concerned for everyone—my brother who was a mechanic, my other younger brother and his wife, my dad and mom, and my youngest brother, who was nine years old. We needed to bounce back. But first, we needed to feed, clothe, shelter, and celebrate Christmas and New Year. We had some plants left from the bankruptcy, and we did have a planting contract with a local hospital that was still pending. So I called the hospital and told them our story and asked if we could perform the project. They agreed. We were back for at least one more project! So my recently married brother and I installed the plants and completed the project. We made $4,500.00. So we divided it up four ways. That went well, but we still needed more to carry us through the winter. So again, my brother and I decided we would search the industry for some ideas. We stumbled upon a greenhouse grower who suggested we sell poinsettias. He gave us a great deal on the plants, and he told us to concentrate on churches. They bought a lot for the holidays. Great idea! So we did, and we made enough money to get us through the winter and into the spring.

We learned all we had to do was be positive and understand this was a minor setback. Keep the faith, and all would turn out well. These hard times proved we could handle anything put before us. We just believed God was testing us, and we didn't want to let him down. We made it through the winter, and now a new hurdle was before us. What were we going to do now? We could start all over. We did it once. We could do it again. But wait, out of nowhere, another twist of fate! Again, a God-driven opportunity was in the making.

I received a phone call, out of the blue, from our old friend, the garden center owner, and he had a proposition for us. So as we were having our spaghetti dinner meeting, we discussed our next steps. I brought up the new proposal just brought up to me a few days ago. I explained I received a phone call from our old friend, the garden center owner. He mentioned he wanted to sell one of his two garden centers, and he was interested in us. I explained to him our situation and that we had no money and the bankruptcy. He understood, but he was still willing to make a deal. So I listened. He was willing to forgo the formal up-front money, and he would help us establish credit with the vendors he used. Plus, we had contacts of our own who would be willing to give us some limited start-up help. I explained to the spaghetti dinner meeting people that we all had talent in the industry. We knew plants and proper installation techniques. We all sold many projects, and three of the four of us were very retail-oriented because of our shoe sales abilities. It was a win-win. A no-brainer or a slam dunk.

After a few days of meetings and discussions, my dad and mom said okay. My brother and his wife were on the fence post and leaning not at this time. He was happy with his mechanic job at that time. My newlywed brother and his wife were on board, and so was my wife and I. So I went to the garden center owner and told him we wanted to move forward with the deal and he could start drawing up the paperwork. As it turned out, my brother that was on the fence post decided not to come on board. I knew it was going to be a loss because of his experience and expertise in the field, but we all respected his decision. So the three of us signed on for a seven-year term. The terms were tough, but we felt we could make it work. We were back in business.

So in March of 1982, we established a retail/wholesale garden center. The first year was a bit of a struggle. We were landscapers from the mid '70s until 1982. So we stocked our garden center with large plants and trees. People would come in, look around, thank us, and leave. We were confused. The stock was beautiful, sizable, and priced right. What could be the problem? So we started to ask our customers, and the majority said, "We are looking for shrubs, but you are carrying mostly bushes, and they are too big for us to put in our vehicles. Your trees are beautiful, but again, they are too big." Our thoughts were, *What? What's the difference between a shrub and a bush?* To us, it meant the same thing. So we asked for clarification. So they would point out what they considered a "bush" and what they considered a "shrub." Now we understood their meanings. The *bush* was a deciduous plant or shrub that loses its leaves in the winter, and a *shrub* was an evergreen and, most of the time, flowering. Ahh, a light bulb went off. So we called our suppliers and changed our direction immediately. Now in business, you must be flexible enough to change in a split second for the improvement of your products and business. Plus, you must listen to your customers, because without them, you have no business. This flexibility and change created a major impact on our business, customers, and bottom line. Now we were on the right path. Things were going well. Lesson learned.

Another lesson, I listened to the previous garden center owner about the correct market we should go after. He strongly urged me to concentrate my advertising dollars in a more affluent area fifteen to twenty miles away from the garden center. I listened, but no one from that area came to the garden center, and we very rarely delivered to the area. At one of our Sunday informal meetings, my father brought up my advertising strategy. His comment was, "These people live too far away. Garden center shoppers want to shop close to home, five miles maybe, not take the fifteen-to twenty-mile trip to us." He said, "Advertise in your own backyard, and the rest will eventually follow. These people have jobs, they have houses with yards, and they have money to spend." I thought for a minute and said, "You're right. I'm going to change it tomorrow." My younger brother agreed. And that was exactly what I did. It was a good thing I had my dad around to keep me on the right path. Again, a win. We immediately saw a positive change. More people came, and we sold more plants. Our bottom line was looking good. And our new customers became "loyal" customers—a goal every business strives for but very few obtain.

Now my dad came up with another idea. I should tell now in his shoe days, my dad was an award winning "window display" expert. Now he was using this mastery with plants and how to display them like no other in the garden center. But later, we were copied on a marginal scale because this technique took time and extra effort. He came up to me, puffing on his nonfiltered Chesterfield cigarette, and said, "If I'm a customer and I walk into this store, I can see everything with a quick look to the right and another to the left. That's not good. We need the customers to walk the garden center and really look at the plants. We need to add some intrigue. So I feel we should not line the plants up smallest to the largest and all the same plant varieties in one spot. We should mix it up a bit. Instead of having the paths in straight, symmetrical lines, we should bend them and identify the paths by lining them on both sides with brick. Plus, we need to get rid of the traditional 'wood mulch' paths and plant mulching in. And we should use shot/pea gravel instead. This would eliminate weeds from growing in the mulch and balled and bur-lapped plants from rooting in the mulch, causing damage to the plant when we need to move it because a customer purchases it. With shot/pea gravel, the plant roots grow but are not entangled in the gravel. They pull out with little or no harm to the plant. Plus, when we sell a plant in the shot/pea gravel, all we need to do is rake the gravel out, and the bed looks great. Now we need to put in the shrubs not in like variety and put plants that complement each other, which will show customers how they blend, making great planting partners. And finally, we should intersperse the trees, pines, and deciduous throughout these new, weaving path beds. This will allow the trees to shade the shrubs in the hotter days, plus they will be watered when the shrubs are watered. The customers will be able to see the trees 360 degrees in full view. This would also allow the trees to grow more symmetrical." We did all his ideas, and wow, what a success! Word got out about our unique look, and customers gravitated to our garden center. It became a must-see destination. Customers' children referred to us as a "fun park/playground." As time passed, other garden centers took note and started to marginally follow our unique look. Fortunately for us, they were all in other states.

Also, in our earlier years, we were targets for community and school fund donations. Here's one fund donation that stood out in our early years. Two older women walked into our establishment asking for a donation in support for the local high school football team's summer camp lunches. Every day there was another cause we were asked to fund. It frustrated me. But I held my frustrated emotions in check. I asked, "How much do you want?" Their answer, as all the others seeking a monetary donation, was, "Whatever you can give." Now the pressure was on me. I couldn't say "No, I don't want to donate" because it was for school. And I couldn't give a little. If I did either of the two, our garden center would be marked as selfish, noncaring, and cheap. So I wrote a check out for $250.00, which was what most people expected. I handed them the check. They both looked at me, kind of nondescript, and they sighed or moaned. Oh no, was it too low? Did I make a mistake? So I asked, "Is there a problem? Do you need more?" In my mind, I was thinking, *What the heck!* But again, I showed concern, not frustration.

Finally, one of them spoke up. She said, "Oh no, this is much more than we expected. You just paid 100 percent for all the lunches for the entire week." I was now thinking, *Darn. I can't change my mind now.* The other lady now spoke up and said, "We are going to put a giant banner up in the high school cafeteria saying all lunches were sponsored by the garden center for all to see." Now I was happy. That was a real surprise. And what a lucky, nice, beneficial turn of events. So I told the two ladies that we would sponsor football camp lunches every year. They did not need to look any further. All we asked was that they put a banner up in the cafeteria every year. Many opportunities came up throughout the years similar to this one.

Another notable event was an opportunity for the local township. They were having a community day celebration with a 5K race, and they were looking for sponsors. We offered to sponsor the 5K race, and we would supply and print all their T-shirts to be given to all participants. If they would let us, all we wanted was to be the sole name on the back of the 5K race T-shirt as the sole sponsor. They agreed.

One more community/school event I'll mention at this time was our sponsorship for a holiday poinsettia sale. The kids were having a holiday dance that they needed to raise money for. A few parents approached us and asked if we would participate in the event. We suggested that the students could have a poinsettia sale. We would supply the poinsettias at a very deep discount, and we suggested they sell them at our retail price. This way, the purchaser would be more inclined to buy off the students and not the retail stores. They were excited and agreed to the sale. The sale was a raving success. They sold over nine hundred poinsettias. The students made enough money to pay for their dance and put money in their account for another project. So many poinsettias sold that the school did not have enough room to store them. So we offered to distribute the poinsettias through our store. They agreed, and all went well. Other such events happened, and I will highlight one or two as I develop my growth and qualifications.

In 1986, we were looking for a new, fresh marketing strategy, which we stumbled on through a garden center trade magazine. It was called Crape Myrtle Days. It was a very unique and involved marketing event. We actually canceled our first event in 1987 because we were not totally prepared. Not to copy the event and the fact that crape myrtle did not grow in our area, we named it Beach Party Weekend, giving off a *Jersey Shore*, "California fun in the sun" vibe. It was a very festive weekend.

In 1988, our inaugural celebration, we were totally prepared. We had our youngest brother and his band playing beach songs. We brought in white sand and made a beach. We rented a Pepsi trailer and sold hot dogs, homemade pizza by the slice, chips, and Pepsi products. A vintage car or two or three were displayed along with some Dune bikes and nonalcoholic beer etc. We made carnival games for all to play. And when the band was not playing, we piped in beachy music. We ordered special T-shirts for all the employees to wear. When you won at the carnival games, you won a prize with our name on it. But that wasn't the purpose of the event. The ultimate goal was to have fun, show appreciation to our loyal customers, and make money.

Here's how it worked. For every $10.00 a customer spent at the garden center from January of that year until the day before the beach party, you earned one sand dollar. They were paper dollars that had a value of $1.00, redeemable at the Beach Party Weekend. On Beach Party Weekend, these sand dollars became real dollars, up to 50 percent off anything we sold. We picked the third weekend in July to have the Beach Party Weekend. Traditionally, July was the slowest month of our season, and the third weekend was the slowest weekend. This held true for all garden centers in our climactic region. Any garden center at this time of the year was lucky if they grossed $3,000.00 over the entire weekend. The first year, we grossed $16,000.00 over this weekend. Not bad for the time of the year, and we were getting rid of stock others were sitting on. Each year, we would add an event or two to the beach party as it became a banner event. For example, we had an artist who painted beautiful animals on smooth rocks, Uncle Sam on stilts made animals and other items out of balloons, and a hot-air balloon tethered up 125 feet and came back down, to name a few. By 1994, we were grossing a cool $87,000.00 in the three-day weekend. Now we're talking. This weekend surpassed our monthly total for August. All our loyal customers took it as customer appreciation weekend because you needed sand dollars to receive a discount. No sand dollars, no discount. You had to pay retail. The entire weekend was all hands on deck, plus some of our employees' family and friends. Those three days, we were packed from open to close. By Sunday, we were all exhausted. So we closed at 6:00 p.m. and had a celebratory party of our own.

As time and the event grew, we had to close early the Thursday before because people would try to jump the gun and spend their sand dollars early. Also, as the event grew, we stocked up so the customers had a larger variety to pick from. Our largest vendor thought we were nuts. He said, "No one stocks up in July, and you are stocking pretty heavy. You can't be doing that kind of business." We said, "Stop by and see for yourself." Fred said, "I will, and if you're that busy, I'll stay the whole day." We agreed. On Friday, Fred pulled up, and we were packed with people, cars, and trucks everywhere. They were parking on the road and neighboring parking lots. Our delivery people were lined up, getting loaded, etc. Fred said, "Give me a shirt." Now we also had residual sales. Customers who could not make the weekend were able to spend their sand dollars the next week without all the fun and events. It even happened that customers would come out a week or two before the event to check on things they wanted, to see if they were still available or to plan their approach and make decisions on what they wanted. In other words, strategize. Some would come in and buy more because they did not have enough sand dollars to get 50 percent off. Plus, on Beach Party Weekend, customers who didn't spend all their sand dollars would hand a complete stranger their leftover sand dollars for them to use. We loved that. We built our worst month and our worst weekend into a banner month, rivaling our best month and weekend.

We had a similar event around Halloween called Hobbly Gobbly Weekend. We had a pumpkin patch, cornstalk maize, carnival games, bobbing for apples, etc. Prizes again were all with the garden center name, and it was okay. It was not as wild as the Beach Party Weekend. At this event, we were not bringing in any new stock.

We truly wanted to get rid of all we had. Picking was slim, and people were ready for a break and the pending holidays and not working in their yards, except to rake leaves. Winter was on its way, and we were really preparing for Christmas and snow removal.

Now let's talk dollars and cents for the Beach Party Weekend and Hobbly Gobbly Weekend. The unique thing is, if you take the customers' purchases for the entire year, including the ones it took to earn the sand dollars and include the Beach Party Weekend purchases, they used their sand dollars for a maximum discount of 50 percent. The yearly discount is only 10 percent. And the 10 percent discount decreased if their discount was not at the max 50 percent discount. And we had a lot of those. Note, every beach party had a different theme and color.

We also made our own twelve-month calendar of events. All our events were unique, and every month had a different theme. We gave the calendars out at the Beach Party Weekend because it was the largest concentration of people we had in a short period of time. After the beach party, we placed them on the counters so the customers could pick them up. Of course, the calendar started in August of that year through July of the next year, when the customers could pick up a new one at that year's beach party.

On Mother's Day, hanging basket extravaganza, we gave every female a long-stemmed carnation and wished them a "Happy Mother's Day." We had our children and our employees' children help in the distribution of the carnations. One year I had this crazy idea. Instead of giving out a $0.35 carnation, we'd up the game and give out a $1.50 spaghetti server with our name on it! Boy, was I wrong! Yikes! All the women felt the spaghetti server meant work. So back to the $0.35 carnations. And we never looked back. We also had an area for dads and kids where they could make Mom a small flower arrangement. Now everyone liked that. We took care of Mom; now we need to take care of Dad. On Father's Day every year, we gave out a different-colored baseball cap. This was okay, but not as enthusiastic as Mother's Day. Dads had other things in mind instead of going to a garden center, which meant work.

At Christmas, we had sleigh rides, pony rides, and pictures with Santa. And if you bought a tree from us, you received a garden center collector ornament. Each year, we had a different ornament. Customers would come in and tell us they made up a smaller tree, calling it the garden center tree.

During high school prom season for the local school districts, we loaned flowering and evergreen plants to use as backdrops for the prom pictures. This was a free service. The students, parents, teachers, or school employees would choose the plants they wanted. We would help load them on a truck and explain the care requirements for the plants. All we asked was they be returned unharmed. Proms were generally held during our peak season. At this time, we had an abundant supply of excellent plants. They were in bloom, and the evergreens were in excellent shape. So loaning them out for a weekend didn't hurt our sales any. The positive response was outstanding. Students, parents, grandparents, and school staff all responded positively. The plants always came back in excellent shape. We even received copies of some of the pictures to display on our bulletin board for all to see.

We developed a kids club, similar to McDonald's and other national customers. It was free to join. When you joined, you would receive a postcard in the mail to visit the store to pick up an official T-shirt, membership card, and coloring book. Plus, we sent out a monthly kids club newsletter with educational information and a project or two that the member and an adult could complete together. The name of the club was Cool Beans Kids Club. To our surprise, the T-shirts became a status symbol at the local swimming pools. The kids would wear them as a top cover when not in the water. The shirts were yellow with blue and green stencils of three cool green beans smiling and having fun, plus the name of the club and our name on it. The reason I mentioned the colors was because when an elementary school year ended in our area, they would have fun events and competitions for the students. The classes would pick one of the US states as their team's name. The students would research their respective state and, on stage, present a program, along with the competition. Well, I received a phone call from one teacher requesting if we would be interested in donating some Cool Beans T-shirts to their team. He further explained that their state was Pennsylvania, and the Cool Beans colors were the state's colors. We, of course, agreed. Plus, we agreed the teachers in the group would receive Cool Beans shirts too. The Pennsylvania team won the competition. They had their pictures taken and put on the front page of a local newspaper wearing, you guessed it, Cool Beans T-shirts!

To backtrack a bit, the Cool Beans Kids Club did not start out first. It was a brainchild of our initial plan, which was "Seed for Kids." We would send out request forms to local elementary schools, offering them a science project. We would supply each student individually packaged one-seed pack, peat pot, and directions on how to plant and maintain their plants. We would also supply the teachers with enough planting medium to handle all the students' needs, and they would receive their own kits. The teachers liked the concept and Seeds for Kids was off and running. Every year, more and more schools and students wanted to participate in the Seeds for Kids program.

A year or two into this program, we wanted to enhance it. So after some brainstorming, we came up with the Cool Beans Kids Club. We already had an obvious base for the club. We placed club applications in the students' seed packets. But before we did that, we asked for permission, and when it was granted, we installed the applications. In a very short time, we had twelve thousand club members! If you remember, we sent out postcards addressed to the club member to stop by the garden center to pick up their T-shirt, membership card, and coloring book. And how do first graders through sixth graders get to the garden center? Right. From an adult or two or four who had a driver's license. Plus, as all parents or guardians know, when a young person receives mail, it's exciting. Plus, if they get something they need to pick up, well, the requesting doesn't end until the deed is completed. Sounds kind of clever. Yep, you're right. It was clever.

I left one thing out. On the Cool Beans club members' birthday, we would send out another postcard informing them that we had a present for them. All they had to do was come in with the postcard to pick it up. Clever again. The birthday gift was a free indoor plant. When the parents or guardian came in and found out their present was an indoor plant, they would kind of get an attitude, kind of like, "Wow, let's see this thing," expecting to see a tiny two-inch plant pot or something. Well, to their surprise, I made a deal with a Florida grower, and the present was a mature six-inch or one-gallon plant. And we had at least one hundred plants to choose from. Well, now the adult attitude would change immediately. They would start picking out the birthday person's gift. What a warm and fuzzy, positive feeling for all. Of course, while the parent or guardian and the birthday kid were at the garden center two times now, they would walk the center and get more familiar with the garden center and cheerful staff.

We took the Cool Beans Kids Club one step further. One of our staff members was a seamstress, so she made a Cool Beans costume, and we started prescheduled school visits and elementary-level talks. Plus, she made a Cool Beans statue for the store where children could reach into its belly and get a piece or two of candy.

Not to leave the adults out, we also developed a club for them. This was for all the homeowners or people who wanted to join. We called it the Weekend Warriors Club. This was not a free club. This club cost $39.99 to join, and for this membership fee, the member received a binder full of helpful information on measurement, plant installation and care, proper plant pruning, and insects and plant pests and how to control them, among many other bits of information. We would also send out updates and new information to be placed in the binder. Along with the binder, each member received a T-shirt, a sweatband, and a graduated discount card. The more you purchased, the larger your discount would be, up to 30 percent off. We also gave you advance notice on the advertised and unadvertised happenings.

In-store pamphlets and handouts were also always available in our information center. Our information center was named PMS (Plant Maintenance Services). Yes, this was on purpose. Most customers were amused with the title PMS Information Center. Plus, customers would spend time in the center reading and collecting pamphlets and asking educational questions. So the PMS Information Center was always kept well stocked. The center had the nuts and bolts about specific plant care and installation, lawn care and installation, pest and fungus control, and proper pruning techniques, plus specific care for plants that were hard to grow or maintain and seasonal plants such as poinsettias.

As a company rule for our salespeople, if we sold a plant, grass seed, flower, tree, edging, etc., they would take you to the PMS Information Center, give you all the information you needed, and explain the proper planting and care process. And if the customer was interested, they would take you to the products area and help pick out the necessary items. They would ensure a positive experience. This process educated the customer and created additional sales for the company. One example, and we were called on this a few times, was when a customer would buy an $8.00 plant, and we would sell them twenty-dollars' worth of soil, fertilizer, and a water retention product to plant it properly and keep it alive. They would comment on the fact that they could buy two more plants, so if this one died, they could have two more tries at a successful outcome. We would both have a chuckle, but they always bought the extra planting material.

We also added a PMS insurance plan for newly purchased plants. It was very similar to an appliance or tool insurance or warranty plan.

As we grew in stature, we were asked to sit on the founding boards of Growise and Trustworthy.

Both associations were formed to help independent garden centers and hardware stores to combat the mass merchants. The members of each association would band together, having greater buying power, to combat the large-box stores. We developed television advertising, sales pamphlets, and some events.

We also offered our own private credit card. It was funded through a company named Beneficial Finance. At first, it was hard to get off the ground, because why would a customer get a card that they could only use at our store? So we gave our employees $1.50 for every person they signed up. It was called an incentive. Once the customer used the card, we were guaranteed payment from Beneficial, and we were out of the picture for billing and collections.

Not to leave anyone out, we started another club and named it the Elite Club. This was geared to landscapers, municipalities, and larger corporations. Plus, if they participated, all their employees were entitled to join, and they, too, could receive discounts. Each group or category had their own specific discounts and parameters.

Back in 1990, we started a regional cable television marketing program. At this time, cable television in our area was new, and advertising rates were reasonable. The fact that you had a choice to pick your area of concentration helped in the pricing and value. This actually made us look larger than we actually were. One of our first networks was CNN. At the time, CNN was a relatively unknown upstart news channel. But on August 2, 1990, guess what happened? Desert Storm! And CNN grew in notoriety by covering the war 24-7.

At the time, our cable television agent did not sell all the CNN spots, so when this happened, there was no dead space in the advertising slots where they put the advertisers that bought spots on what they called the rotation, and even if you only paid for four spots, you would receive more spots to fill the void at no extra charge to you. And that was exactly what happened. As time went on, we marketed our company more. We were asked if we would do a testimonial about cable television and its value. So we decided to do it. In the middle of the garden center, I sat with plants around me, and on the screen, in the testimonial, was my name and the garden center's name. This commercial was aired on every cable television channel and in the entire master region for weeks, maybe months. One of my friends and a loyal customer jokingly said, "If I see your face on television one more time, I'm going to throw my shoe through the television." We had a good laugh.

As time went on, the garden center grew. Many people started to know us as a destination. We were becoming established in our community and surrounding communities. Our customers were not only satisfied customers, but many had become loyal customers. So we felt we became of age for our next marketing step. For the past couple of years, I was watching a commercial from a local franchise restaurant that they ran only during the Christmas season. The commercial had no one talking. It was an animated, undecorated Christmas tree that bent down and picked up a glowing yellow star and placed it on top of the tree. As the tree was straightening, glowing yellow bulbs would appear. And at the bottom of the scene, their name would appear. Throughout the commercial, light, festive music was playing. End of commercial. Wow, what an impact!

So we secured the services of a local graphic arts company to create our animated commercial. It was of a large deciduous tree sleeping with no leaves on its branches. The tree slowly twisted and creaked. Its eyes fluttered. Leaves started to pop on the tree. Grass started to grow. Flowers bloomed. A rabbit and squirrel hopped into the scene. Birds flew in and landed on some of the branches. The tree woke up, eyes wide open, and started to wave a branch that resembled a magic wand, and our name, address, and phone number appeared on the screen. End of commercial. While all that was going on, light and spring-like music, creaking noises, and bird sounds were happening. There were no spoken words. It was a real hit. People loved the commercial.

Moving on, we were mentioned by a large national box store in one of their commercials, which meant people were starting to notice us. The commercial read, "For a pack of annual flowers, the garden center price, $2.49 per pack; Hechinger's price, $1.99." A great deal of our loyal customers came in concerned about how we were going to handle this negative ad. I had already commissioned my youngest brother to make up an in-store sign that read, "Thank you, Hechinger. The garden center breaking the chains." And on the sign were two Hulk-like fisted hands with large chains in each hands, and the chains were snaping from the force of the Hulk-like hands. Then the loyal customers would give a sigh of relief and chuckle. "I knew you would make a positive out of a negative." And then they would proceed to shop.

We also had an hour-long radio show at a local radio station. It was a call-in show. It was about plants, pests, cures, and anything else the callers wanted to talk about in the landscape/gardening arena. Some people would call in with their home remedies, experiences, etc. We had our own commercials throughout our segment and, at other times, during the week. The commercials were cute. They were two chipmunks talking about gardening, landscaping, and the garden center and their helpful staff. They were cute and informative.

Within the garden center, we opened a floral shop run by a very talented florist. In my eyes, she was the best in the area. She kept the shop running like a well-oiled machine. In the process, she trained several young ladies into being masters of the trade. Her famous saying was, "We have to bap these floral arrangements out." I always got a chuckle out of that. If she had a problem with me or other things within the floral area or even the garden center in general, she would always say, "Paul, cooler." Then I would know I was in for an earful. But I kind of liked the "cooler" time. It was good bonding, and we always solved the problem.

With a garden center as a base, the floral center was unique. We had more walk-in trade than a stand-alone florist where they mainly depended on the phone or wire service for business.

Our primary floral marketing was through the garden center. But we also had other marketing objectives. One idea was, we would pick out a local business on a daily basis and send what we named a day-brightener bouquet with a card saying, "Hope you have a brighter day. Compliments of the floral shop at the garden center."

We also developed a Floral Arrangement Club. There was no charge to join the club. The idea behind it was, you could schedule floral arrangements to be delivered on specific dates that you pick for any upcoming personal event. We broke it down like this: you could purchase three, six, nine, or twelve floral arrangements at a predetermined price and date, and our floral department would send them out with a card that you determined the saying. One occasion that stuck out in my mind was that of a local police officer. He signed up to have the girls send an arrangement to his wife for their anniversary. So on the designated date, our floral staff sent out this beautiful arrangement with a card he had made months earlier. He came rushing into our store saying his wife received an anniversary bouquet from us, and he wanted to know who sent it. We told him it was from him and he had signed up for three arrangements throughout the year. He was relieved, and he mentioned he had forgotten their anniversary, so we saved his butt. We all laughed and went on with our day.

The floral shop also helped even out the seasonal valleys we encountered season after season. Christmas, Valentine's, St. Patrick's, Easter, and winter floral classes helped cash flow, along with our snowplowing services.

The floral girls also went to hotels and large businesses, canvassing for weekly floral arrangements for their lobbies and table arrangements for their events, such as corporate meetings or weddings. This led to the floral department doing Christmas decorating at some major hotels and office buildings in our market area. The girls also went to funeral homes and offered floral packages funeral directors could offer.

The floral girls, with the help of my youngest brother, would design and send out custom-designed Christmas cards. We also sent out custom-labeled wine and six-dozen holiday cookies made by one of our landscape supervisors to all our commercial customers.

In season, we developed a weekend bulk delivery service. The weekend was our busiest time for deliveries to the DIYers and landscapers. So we acted like it was a normal weekday and scheduled our three-weekday trucks as much as we could. But on the weekend, we would have five trucks ready to go. The three would be scheduled, but the two added trucks were open to take on new orders or simply help out with the existing orders until we received more orders. This way, we could satisfy the scheduled customers and the last-minute customers. Many times, our prices were higher than another supplier. But the fact that we could deliver that day and many times within a short period of time, the customer would gladly pay us the extra cost. Our trucks would run from 7:00 a.m. until 8:00 p.m. on Saturday and from 8:00 a.m. to 6:00 p.m. on Sunday.

Our philosophy throughout the company was, "Do what others don't and capitalize on it."

As the company grew, we had to involve our employees more in our goals and philosophies. So we developed an employee handbook with the usual stuff along with our short-term and long-term goals, a mission statement and our philosophies, and our promise to the employee and customers. We also created specific employee position descriptions. Store personnel was schooled on proper customer greetings, etiquette, grooming, and appearance.

Each garden center employee was assigned specific areas inside and outside to maintain neatly and cleanly. Their inside responsibilities were to maintain specific shelf areas by keeping them dust-free, fronted, and assigned shelf talkers (my Keebler cookies training). Their outside specific areas of responsibilities were to keep their areas weed-free, stocked orderly, pruned, watered, and fertilized (my shoe days training). But first and foremost, they were to greet and assist any and all customers with all their needs. We had a telephone rule, another front door, that it was to be answered within three rings. So we strategically placed telephones around the store for that purpose. Plus, all of us were scheduled to clean the restrooms daily, another front door, starting with me being the first to clean, then the other owners, then the department managers, and on down. It added up that I was cleaning the restroom once every eighteen days. We had grounds maintenance and contracting divisions, plus a landscape architect on staff. We developed what we called a sidewalk design for the DIYers who wanted to buy today and install today. We trained all the garden center staff on this concept.

That brings us to our extensive employee training at the garden center as well as in the field. We spent extra time with all our supervisors in each division. We taught our homegrown practices of store procedures, proper delegation, and people dynamics, to name a few.

Now in closing this qualifications portion, I would like to explain our marketing philosophy. We did not feel we needed to market ourselves over other companies in our field of expertise. We were after people's discretionary or expendable cash. Let me explain. Everyone has dedicated cash, for example, house payment, rent, vehicle, utilities, savings, credit cards, etc. And what is left over is discretionary or expendable cash. This cash is for entertainment, such as going to the movies, vacations, amusement park, swimming, eating out, or in our case, going to the garden center. Now that's where we concentrated the majority of our marketing monies. Plus, our goal was to be "part of the community," not just be a business in the community. And we accomplished that through football camp, prom flowers, poinsettia sales, day-brightener bouquets, Beach Party Weekend, etc. Also, when we added on to the garden center (expanded), many customers would come in and say "What are we doing now?" with excitement in their voices. Now the key word here is *we*.

Now back to the purpose of this accounting—my qualifications and ability to offer constructive suggestions.

Remember Eck, my friend, who wanted me to help a struggling garden center out by offering some constructive suggestions? I feel I have accomplished my qualifications and ability.

Well, moving on, I visited their establishment, and as I pulled into their parking lot, my critical eye or eye for detail immediately kicked into gear. I started recording notes into my mini tape recorder. After a few minutes in the parking lot, I went into the store and again started with my critical eye or eye for detail, noting everything and everyone I came into contact with. I spent forty-five minutes to an hour throughout the garden center. I carefully walked up and down the aisles, looking at displays and cleanliness. I ventured into their restroom. I listened for the telephone. I picked up any and all written promotional or educational information they had lying around. I walked through their plant areas. I also snuck in their Employees Only areas, all the while talking my observations into the tape recorder. When I was satisfied I had seen enough, I casually walked out and returned to my office. There, I listened to my tape and started to write notes on my observations. To my surprise, I was developing a "business analysis." This was getting exciting. So I made a list of four major categories for the physical plant: (1) exterior, (2) interior, (3) staff, and (4) marketing. Under each category, I listed what I saw and what I would do if I were the owner of this establishment. I was walking in their shoes with my ideas.

This started to paint a picture. So I created a chart listing all the categories and their details or bullet points.

1. Physical plant
    1. Exterior
        a. Signage (fresh, crisp, readable, helpful, professional)

    b. Visibility (open, cluttered, accessible, hidden)

    c. Cleanliness (colorful, filled with weeds, manicured)

    d. Neatness: (trimmed, edged, manicured)

    e. Drive/entry (open, defined, welcoming, visible, paved, graveled, with potholes, accessible)

    f. Parking (accessible, paved, gravel, with potholes, visible, convenient)

    g. Traffic flow (well-defined, patterned, smooth)

    h. Structures (clean, painted, good covers, good canopies)

    i. Displays (attractive, inviting, clean, changing)

    j. Other (pets, water items, puddles, potholes, trash, trash cans, potting area, debris, loading area's appearance)

2. Interior

    a. Signage (fresh, crisp, readable, helpful, professional)

    b. Organization (departmentalized)

    c. Cleanliness (colorful, trash, dirt, dust)

d. Neatness (debris off the floor, stock put in proper place)
e. Aisles (wide, open, clear, narrow, closed, cluttered)
f. Entry (open, defined, welcome, well lit, clean, cluttered)
g. Traffic flow (well-defined, patterned, departmentalized)
h. Structures (shelves, displays, tables, floor, painted, dust-free, dirt free, changing)
i. Checkout counters (accessible, open, cluttered, staffed)
j. Restrooms (clean, neat, open, well stocked, dirty, smelly)
k. Displays (attractive, inviting, clean, neat, well stocked, changing, end caps)
l. Reference areas (well stocked with educational fliers and books, knowledgeable staff on hand to assist with questions and problems)
m. Other (pets, water items, puddles, tripping hazards, trash, trash cans, craft areas, boxes, broken items)

3. Staff
    1. Grooming (hair, beard, hygiene, teeth)
    2. Dress (uniform; neat, clean, hole-free shirt or pants; work boots; tennis shoes; sandals; socks)

First impression:
    3. Approach (aggressive, timid, lazy, you approach or they approach)
    4. First contact (timely, cheerful, polite, helpful, concerned, suggestive)
    5. Greeting (usual ["Can I help you?], creative ["Hi, my name is ___. How may I be of service today?"], how long before greeting)
    6. Attitude (upbeat, cheerful, concerned, helpful)
    7. Knowledge (knows what they're talking about, knows how to get the answer)
    8. Communication skills (can get point across in an understandable manner)
    9. Understandable direction (knows subject well enough to communicate in any level of expertise or knows someone who can help

with the problem and gets them to assist ASAP)

10. Telephone etiquette (the other front door, human vs. machine, amount of rings before answering, on-hold length, help and concern for caller)

4. Marketing

1. Hours of operation (evening and weekend hours, a.m. hours, p.m. hours)

2. Open year-round or seasonal (full- or part-time enterprise, off-season sale items, diversification to counter seasonality)

3. Stock quality and quantity (Does the stock reflect care, knowledge, and professionalism? Does the product satisfy the needs of the customer?)

4. Stock depth and product mix (satisfy customer needs)

5. Stands behind product, services, and word (guarantee, do what you say you are going to do, keep promises, do not make promises you cannot keep)

6. Know and study customer needs (learn; study and understand

your customer shopping trends; marina, custom, townhouse, or apartment within a five-mile radius of the establishment; target customer base)

7. Knows competition (visit study, understand your competition, posture yourself and compliment yourself with them [*you are all after expendable cash*])

8. Extra services (delivery, design, installation)

9. Focused advertising (*do not go toe to toe with the mass merchants* [go *side by side*]; mass merchant is mass advertising; independent is focused [pinpoint], mailing lists developed from your own customer base, subliminal advertising [schools, community, professional organizations, etc.], in-store advertising, signage, handouts)

10. Subliminal advertising (schools, churches, nonprofit organization, community involvement, events)

11. Entertain others (something for all the members of the shopping

experience [e.g., moms, dads, seniors, kids, events])
12. Handouts (listen to customer questions, print handouts for these items and other items of interest)
13. Staff (see "Staff," item 3)
14. Appearance (see "Physical Plant")

Do what others do not and do it well!

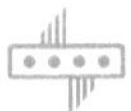

Business Analysis

A. Physical Plant	Customer-Friendly	Owner-Friendly	Why
1. Exterior a. Signage			
b. Visibility			
c. Cleanliness			
d. Neatness			
e. Drive/entry			
f. Parking			
g. Traffic Flow			
h. Structures			
i. Displays			
j. Other			

A. Physical Plant	Customer-Friendly	Owner-Friendly	Why
1. Interior			
a. Signage			
b. Organization			
c. Cleanliness			
d. Neatness			
e. Aisles			

f. Entry		
g. Traffic flow		
h. Structures		
i. Displays		
j. Checkout counters		
k. Restrooms		
l. Reference area		

B. Staff	Customer-Friendly	Owner-Friendly	Why
1. Grooming			
2. Dress			
3. First impression			
4. Approach			
5. First contact			
6. Greeting			
7. Attitude			
8. Knowledge			
9. Communication skills			
10. Understandable direction			
11. Telephone etiquette			

C. Marketing	Customer-Friendly	Owner-Friendly	Why
1. Hours of operation			
2. Open year-round or seasonal			
3. Stock quality and quantity			
4. Stock depth and prod-uct mix			
5. Stands behind product and word			
6. Knows stud-ies customer needs			
7. Knows competition			
8. Extra services			
9. Focused advertising			
10. Subliminal advertising			
11. Entertains others			
12. Handouts			

In each category or bullet point, I classified them as customer-friendly, owner-friendly, and why.

After developing the guidelines and charts, I proceeded to analyze my findings. I then wrote up what I felt was a solution or the steps necessary to correct their shortcomings. I also included their positives. Upon completion of the newly formed analysis, Eck made an appointment for the both of us to meet with the garden center owner, only to have him cancel the appointment. We attempted several times after the initial cancellation with no success. So we finally decided to simply mail the analysis to him, which resulted in no action on his part whatsoever. I was not disillusioned. I knew I made something of value, and over the years, I have analyzed other businesses with these same guidelines and charts with great success. When they implemented the recommended changes, they reaped the benefits. Not everyone made all the changes. So the successes varied. This analysis is simple and can be performed by an open-minded, visual person with an understanding of what it takes to make a business work and, quite possibly, be a standout in their industry. All you need is a "critical eye" or "an eye for detail" and to give an honest analysis of their business or that of a friend or acquaintance.

Educational and Inspirational Books That Influenced My Business Thoughts and Philosophies

1. *Customer Satisfaction Is Worthless, Customer Loyalty Is Priceless* by Jeffrey Gitomer
2. *The Sales Bible* by Jeffrey Gitomer
3. *Who Moved My Cheese?* by Spencer Johnson, MD
4. *Peaks and Valleys* by Spencer Johnson, MD
5. *Fish* by Stephen C. Lundin, PhD; Harry Paul; and John Christensen
6. *Raving Fans* by Ken Blanchard and Sheldon Bowles
7. *Whale Done!* by Ken Blanchard
8. *Gung Ho!* by Ken Blanchard and Sheldon Bowles

9. *Full Steam Ahead!* by Ken Blanchard and Jesse Stoner
10. *The Leadership Pill* by Ken Blanchard and Marc Muchnick
11. *The One Minute Manager* by Ken Blanchard and Spencer Johnson
12. *Self Leadership and the One Minute Manager* by Ken Blanchard, Susan Fowler, and Laurence Hawkins
13. *The One Minute Manager Builds High Performing Teams* by Ken Blanchard, Donald Carew, and Eunice Parisi-Carew
14. *High Five!* by Ken Blanchard and Sheldon Bowles
15. *Zap the Gaps!* by Ken Blanchard, Dana Robinson, and Jim Robinson
16. *Refire! Don't Retire* by Ken Blanchard and Morton Shaevitz
17. *Leadership by the Book* by Ken Blanchard, Bill Hybels, and Phil Hodges
18. *Trust Works!* by Ken Blanchard, Cynthia Olmstead, and Martha Lawrence
19. *The Secret* by Ken Blanchard and Mark Miller
20. *Mission Possible* by Ken Blanchard and Terry Waghorn
21. *The Winning Attitude* by John C. Maxwell

22. *Developing the Leaders around You* by John C. Maxwell
23. *Becoming a Person of Influence* by John C. Maxwell
24. *Good Leaders Ask Great Questions* by John C. Maxwell
25. *Leadership Secrets of Attila the Hun* by Wess Roberts, PhD
26. *You Can't Send a Duck to Eagle School* by Mac Anderson
27. *Growing Dreams* by Jim Paluch
28. *Peanut Butter and Jelly Management* by Chris and Reina Komisarjevsky
29. *Winning Ways* by Dick Lyles
30. *Made to Stick* by Chip Heath and Dan Heath
31. *Please Don't Just Do What I Tell You!* by Bob Nelson
32. *Fred Factor* by Mark Sanborn
33. *Where's Your Wow?* by Robyn Spizman and Rick Frishman
34. *Catch! A Fishmonger's Guide to Greatness* by Cyndi Crowther and the Crew of World-Famous Pike Place Fish
35. *Purple Cow* by Seth Godin
36. *The Big Moo* by the Group of 33, edited by Seth Godin
37. *How Full Is Your Bucket?* by Tom Rath and Donald O. Clifton, PhD

53. *If It Ain't Broke…Break It!* by Robert Kriegel and Louis Patler
54. *Eckerd: Finding the Right Prescription* by Jack Eckerd and Charles Paul Conn
55. *American Generalship* by Edgar F. Puryear Jr.
56. *The Wisdom of the Native Americans, Including the Soul of an Indian and Other Writings of Ohiyesa and the Great Speeches of Chief Red Jacket, Chief Joseph, and Chief Seattle*, compiled and edited By Kent Nerburn
57. *The 80/20 Principle* by Richard Koch
58. *Profitable Garden Center Management* by Louis Berninger
59. *How to Think like Leonardo Da Vinci* by Michael J. Gelb
60. *Smash the Funnel* by Eric Keiles and Mike Lieberman
61. *In Search of Excellence* by Thomas J. Peters and Robert H. Waterman Jr.
62. *Create Your Own Future* by Linda Georgian
63. *The 7 Habits of Highly Effective People* by Stephen R. Covey
64. *Best Boss, Worst Boss* by James B. Miller
65. *Small Giants* by Bo Burlingham
66. *The Wal-Mart Effect* by Charles Fishman
67. *Selling the Invisible* by Harry Beckwith

68. *If Life Is a Game, These Are the Rules* by Cherie Carter-Scott, PhD
69. *Why Employees Don't Do What They're Supposed to Do and What to Do about It* by Ferdinand F. Fournies
70. *On the Road to Sales Mastery* by Ibrahim Elfiky
71. *Good to Great* by Jim Collins
72. *The Spirit of Enterprise* by George Gilder
73. *Self Matters* by Phillip C. McGraw, PhD
74. *Getting Started in Consulting* by Alan Weiss, PhD
75. *Landscape Operations, Management, Methods, and Materials* by Leroy G. Hannebaum
76. *Small Business Answer Book* by Jim Schell
77. *Tom's Balloon 1977* by Wheelabrator-Frye Inc. (annual reports for young people)
78. *The Kingdom of Erd 1978* by Wheelabrator-Frye Inc. (annual reports for young people)
79. *Alice's Big Story 1979* by Wheelabrator-Frye Inc. (annual reports for young people)
80. *The Money Machine 1980* by Wheelabrator-Frye Inc. (annual reports for young people)

81. *The Surrey 1981* by Wheelabrator-Frye
    Inc. (annual reports for young people)
82. And countless trade and professional
    magazines and seminars, where one
    noted speaker I enjoy is Kevin Kehoe

About the Author

Paul Gaglia is originally from Pittsburgh, Pennsylvania. He now resides in Fort Myers, Florida. Paul is a 1973 graduate of Duquesne University. He has served on several business boards, such as Grow Wise and Trustworthy Hardware. He has been in his own business for over fifty years, starting in 1967, while he was in high school through college and beyond. Paul's first start-up business was Gaglia Gardners, to Gaglia Contractors, where the company landscaped the Pittsburgh Zoo, Erie Insurance Corporate headquarters, and all the University of Pittsburgh campuses, to name a few. He was a founding partner of Green Arbor Nurseries and Flamingo Landscape and Supply. Plus, he has helped run several other businesses throughout his career. Paul started out as a dreamer when he was a young boy. He has developed these dreams into realities.

www.ingramcontent.com/pod-product-compliance
Lightning Source LLC
Chambersburg PA
CBHW021121130726
47988CB00003B/1114